DETROIT LIONS:

History of the Detroit Lions and Beyond the Gridiron- The Lions' Impact on Detroit

James D. Tyler

Copyright

All rights reserved. No part of this publication may be reproduced, distributed, or transmitted in any form or by any means, including photocopying, recording, or other electronic or mechanical methods, without the prior written permission of the publisher except in the case of brief quotations embodied in critical reviews and certain other non-commercial uses permitted by the copyright law.

Copyright © James D. Tyler . 2024.

TABLE OF CONTENTS

INTRODUCTION

Part I: From Portsmouth Spartans to Motor City Might

Chapter 1

Birth of a Team: The Story of the Portsmouth Spartans

    1.1 From Humble Beginnings to Motor City Dreams:

    1.2 Playing with Grit and Spirit

    1.3 Early Struggles and a Glimpse of Glory

    1.4 Moving On and Upward: Detroit Awaits

    1.5 A New Chapter Begins

Chapter 2

Roaring into Detroit: The Lions Arrive and Claim Their First Championship

    2.1 From Portsmouth to Pride

    2.2 A Roar Awakens

    2.3 The Rise of Bobby Layne

    2.4 Championship Glory

    2.5 The Layne Era and Beyond

    2.6 A Legacy Forged

Chapter 3

The Bobby Layne Era: A Golden Age of Grit and Glory

    3.1 The Bobby Layne Era: A Golden Age of Grit and Glory

    3.2 The "Madhouse on Madison"

    3.3 Championship Contenders

    3.4 The 1952 Championship: A Legacy Forged

    3.5 Beyond the Trophy

3.6 The End of an Era

3.7 A Legacy of Grit and Glamour

Chapter 4

The 1950s Dynasty: Three Championships and the Rise of Legends

4.1 Beyond Bobby Layne: A Team of Titans

4.2 Doak Walker: The Running Sensation

4.3 Championship Triumphs

4.4 Unforgettable Rivalries

4.5 A Legacy of Excellence

Chapter 5

Post-Championship Pangs: Decades of Ups and Downs

5.1 The Search for Stability

5.2 Glimmers of Hope

5.3 The Curse of Bobby Lane

5.4 The Silverdome Years

5.5 Thanksgiving Tradition

5.6 The 2011 Cinderella Story

5.7 Decades of Ups and Downs, a City That Never Quits

Chapter 6

The Pride of Pontiac: The Silverdome Years and Memorable Moments

6.1 A Stadium Unlike Any Other

6.2 Memorable Moments etched in Blue

6.3 Beyond the Field: A City's Heartbeat

6.4 The End of an Era, the Roar Lives On

Part II: More Than Just Football: The Lions' Impact on Detroit

Chapter 7
Honolulu Blue Brotherhood: The Unbreakable Bond of Lions Nation
- 7.1 One Pride, One Family
- 7.2 Tradition Runs Deep
- 7.3 More Than Wins and Losses
- 7.4 Lions and the City

Chapter 8
Ford Field: From Stadium to Sanctuary
- 8.1 From Conception to Creation
- 8.2 The Roar Evolves
- 8.3 More Than a Game
- 8.4 Sanctuary of Support
- 8.5 Beyond the Gridiron
- 8.6 The Roar that Unites

Chapter 9
Thanksgiving Tradition: A Ritual of Passion and Community
- 9.1 From Roots to Ritual
- 9.2 Evolution of the Feast
- 9.3 Beyond the Gridiron
- 9.4 More Than Just Wins
- 9.5 A Symbol of Detroit's Spirit

Chapter 10
Beyond the Gridiron: The Lions and Detroit's Social Fabric
- 10.1 From Inspiration to Action
- 10.2 Building Bridges and Community
- 10.3 Hope in the Face of Hardship

    10.4 Fueling Resilience and Identity

Chapter 11

The Curse of Bobby Lane: Fact or Fiction? Examining the Legend

    11.1 The Origins of the Curse

    11.2 Fueling the Flames

    11.3 But is it Real?

    11.4 A Catalyst for Reflection

    11.5 Moving Forward

    11.6 Embrace the Roar

Chapter 12

The Coaching Carousel: The Quest for the Perfect Leader

    12.1 A History of Hope and Heartbreak

    12.2 The Challenges of the Hunt

    12.3 Beyond Wins and Losses

    12.4 Lessons from the Lions' Journey

    12.5 Hope on the Horizon

    12.6 Looking Ahead

Part III

Looking Ahead: The Future of the Detroit Lions

Chapter 13

Building Blocks for a New Era: Young Talent and Potential

    13.1 Foundations of Excellence

    13.2 Beyond the Stats

    13.3 The Crucible of Ford Field

    13.4 The Journey Begins

    13.5 Beyond Individual Brilliance

13.6 Dreams Within Reach

Chapter 14

Beyond the Playing Field: Lions and Business in Detroit

14.1 Economic Engine

14.2 Partnerships and Investments

14.3 Community Champions

14.4 Branding Detroit

14.5 Challenges and Opportunities

14.6 More Than Football

Chapter 15

The Road to Redemption: Overcoming Challenges and Achieving Success

15.1 Facing the Giants

15.2 Beyond Individual Heroics

15.3 Building a Legacy

15.4 More Than Wins and Losses

15.5 The Roar Never Dies

Chapter 16

A City and Its Team: Why Detroit Needs the Lions and Lions Need Detroit

16.1 Detroit Needs the Lions

16.2 The Lions Need Detroit

16.3 Beyond the Gridiron

16.4 Mutual Growth and Rejuvenation

16.5 More Than Wins and Losses

Chapter 17

The Roar of Hope: A Look at the Bright Future of the Detroit Lions

17.1 Foundations of Progress
17.2 Beyond the Stats
17.3 The Crucible of Ford Field
17.4 The Roar of a New Era
17.5 Dreams Within Reach
17.6 Beyond Individual Brilliance
17.7 The Lions and Detroit: A Shared Destiny
17.8 The Dawn of a New Dynasty

CHAPTER 18
INSPIRATION, STATISTICS, EVENTS AND COMMUNITY IMPACT

18.1 Notable Players and Statistics for the Detroit Lions (2023-2024 Season)
18.1.1 Offense
18.1.2 Defense
18.2 Special Teams
18.3 Additional Stats
Points per game: 5th in NFL (27.1)

CHAPTER 19
Timeline of Key Events

19.1 Early Years (1928-1945)
19.2 Bobby Layne Era (1946-1958)
19.3 Post-Layne Era (1959-1989)
19.4 Barry Sanders Era (1989-1998)
19.5 Ford Field Era (2002-Present)
18.6 Other Notable Events

CHAPTER 20
Fun Facts and Trivia

20.1 Origins and Nicknames

20.2 Gridiron Greats
20.3 Ford Field Facts
20.4 Unique Traditions
20.5 Random Tidbits
20.6 Inspirational Stories of Lions Fans and Community Impact
20.6.1 Roar of Resilience
20.7 From Gridiron to Playground
20.8 Unsung Heroes in Blue
20.9 Baking for a Brighter Future
20.9.1 From Fans to Changemakers
CONCLUSION

INTRODUCTION

In the heart of America's grittiest metropolis, where pistons pound and steel whispers tales of industry, resides a team woven into the very fabric of the city. This is not just a story of football, but a saga of resilience, triumph, and unwavering community spirit - a chronicle of the Detroit Lions.

From their humble beginnings as the Portsmouth Spartans, clawing their way to gridiron glory, to the roar of their first championship victory echoing through the Motor City streets, the Lions have always been more than just a team. They are a mirror reflecting Detroit's soul, a beacon of hope amidst challenges, and a testament to the unwavering spirit that resides in every blue-collar heart.

Within these pages, we'll not only delve into the electrifying past, reliving the glory days of Bobby Layne's spirals and Barry Sanders' electrifying runs, but also explore the impact the Lions have on Detroit beyond the green expanse of Ford Field. We'll meet the "Honolulu Blue Brotherhood," a passionate fan-base whose loyalty transcends wins and losses, and witness the stadium itself transcend its brick and mortar to become a sanctuary of joy and shared dreams.

This is a story not just about touchdowns and fumbles, but about community outreach, economic revival, and the unifying power of shared passion. We'll meet players who've become Detroit's champions off the field, and fans whose dedication fuels charitable endeavors and inspires hope.

But this is also a story of looking ahead. We'll dissect the "Coaching Carousel," a whirlwind of strategists seeking to unlock the potential that whispers within this storied franchise. We'll examine the young talent poised to write new chapters in the Lions' legacy, and the challenges that lie ahead on the road to the promised land.

This is an invitation to every armchair quarterback, every face painted Honolulu blue, every Detroiter and every sports enthusiast across the globe. It's a chance to immerse yourself in the soul of a city and its team, to understand why the roar of the Lions resonates far beyond the stadium walls, and to believe, like so many others, that the greatest chapter in this epic tale is yet to be written.

So turn the page, step into the heart of Detroit, and prepare to be captivated by the story of the Detroit Lions – a story not just of football, but of a city, its spirit, and the relentless pursuit of victory, both on and off the field.

PART I: FROM PORTSMOUTH SPARTANS TO MOTOR CITY MIGHT

CHAPTER 1

BIRTH OF A TEAM: THE STORY OF THE PORTSMOUTH SPARTANS

1.1 From Humble Beginnings to Motor City Dreams:

During a time before the towering skyscrapers and roaring engines of Detroit's industrial might, in 1928, and in the small Ohio town of Portsmouth, a spark of gridiron passion ignites. A group of businessmen, led by Harry Newman, sees an opportunity to put their town on the map and bring professional football to the Midwest. Thus, the Portsmouth Spartans are born.

1.2 Playing with Grit and Spirit

These weren't the sleek, million-dollar athletes of today. The Spartans were scrappy underdogs, a team of blue-collar workers and college rejects who took to the field with a fierce determination. Their home, Universal Stadium, was far from glamorous - a horseshoe-shaped wooden structure nicknamed "The Shoe," where wind whipped off the Ohio River and crowds huddled for warmth.

1.3 Early Struggles and a Glimpse of Glory

The Spartans' early years were a mix of wins and losses, marked by financial hurdles and the constant fight for survival. Yet, within this struggle, glimpses of greatness shone through. In 1932, under the leadership of the legendary coach Potsy Clark, the Spartans played in the first-ever NFL playoff game, falling to the mighty Chicago Bears. It was a taste of what could be, a hint of the champion's heart beating within this underdog team.

1.4 Moving On and Upward: Detroit Awaits

By 1934, the financial realities of a small-town team became too harsh. Enter George A. Richards, a Detroit radio executive with a vision. He saw the potential in the Spartans and the untapped football market in Detroit, the vibrant and proud Motor City. With a deal struck, the Spartans packed their bags and headed north, leaving behind the banks of the Ohio for the bustling streets of Detroit.

1.5 A New Chapter Begins

The arrival of the Spartans in Detroit was cause for celebration. The city embraced its new team, renaming them the Detroit Lions in a nod to the iconic Detroit Tigers baseball team. A new era was dawning, one filled with the promise of roaring crowds, electrifying victories, and a place in the heart of a city hungry for sporting glory.

The story of the Portsmouth Spartans is more than just about football. It's a testament to the American spirit of perseverance, the power of ambition, and the unwavering belief that even the smallest of sparks can ignite a flame that burns bright for generations to come. In the next chapter, we'll witness the rise of the Detroit Lions, their transformation from underdogs to champions, and the birth of a legacy that continues to inspire today.

Stay tuned for the next chapter, where the roar of the Lions truly begins!

CHAPTER 2

ROARING INTO DETROIT: THE LIONS ARRIVE AND CLAIM THEIR FIRST CHAMPIONSHIP

2.1 From Portsmouth to Pride

On December 16, 1934 Ford Field wasn't even a glint in anyone's eye, but the streets of Detroit were electric. Thousands cram into the rickety wooden stands of Briggs Stadium, anticipation thick in the crisp winter air. The Portsmouth Spartans, now proudly christened the Detroit Lions, are about to play their first-ever game in their adopted city. The opponent? The Green Bay Packers, a gridiron powerhouse.

2.2 A Roar Awakens

The game is a slugfest, a battle of grit and determination. But the Lions, fueled by the roaring Detroit crowd, play with the heart of underdogs who finally belong. In the closing seconds, Dutch Clark throws a game-winning touchdown pass to Ernie Caddel, and the stadium erupts. Detroit has its first Lions victory, a testament to the city's unwavering spirit and the team's newfound identity.

2.3 The Rise of Bobby Layne

The roaring lion wasn't just a mascot; it became a symbol of the team's burgeoning confidence. Enter Bobby Layne, a brash, swaggering quarterback with a gunslinger's arm and a champion's fire in his eyes. Layne arrived in 1948, and the Lions' destiny changed forever.

2.4 Championship Glory

Under Layne's leadership, the Lions became a force to be reckoned with. Their offensive fireworks, known as the "Madhouse on Madison," tore through defenses. In 1952, the magic culminated in the most thrilling season in Detroit Lions history. Facing the New York Giants in the NFL Championship Game, the Lions trailed 19-17 with seconds left. Then, Layne, facing a fourth down and desperate for a win, unleashed a legendary pass known as the "Throw the Darn Ball to Me!" catch. Wide receiver Jim Patton hauled it in, and the city of Detroit erupted in a frenzy. The Lions were champions, and their roar had reached its peak.

2.5 The Layne Era and Beyond

The years that followed were a rollercoaster of triumphs and challenges. The Layne era saw further playoff appearances and legendary moments like the "Thanksgiving Day Massacre" victory over the Green Bay Packers. But injuries and controversy eventually forced Layne's departure, leaving the city with a bittersweet mix of championship memories and "what ifs."

2.6 A Legacy Forged

Yet, the legacy of the 1950s Lions remained an indelible mark on Detroit's heart. They had shown the city what it meant to compete at the highest level, to claw through adversity, and to roar with pride. They had tasted championship glory, proving that even a team built in a small

Ohio town could become the toast of the Motor City.

The next chapter in the Lions' saga takes us through the golden age of the 1950s, the era of Bobby Layne's magic and Detroit's first taste of gridiron glory. We'll meet the legends who defined this era, relive the thrill of championship victories, and understand the impact these roaring Lions had on a city yearning for hope and triumph.

CHAPTER 3

THE BOBBY LAYNE ERA: A GOLDEN AGE OF GRIT AND GLORY

3.1 The Bobby Layne Era: A Golden Age of Grit and Glory

The 1950s in Detroit were a time of booming industry, soaring skyscrapers, and most importantly, roaring Lions. This was the era of Bobby Layne, a swaggering gunslinger whose arm and attitude redefined the quarterback position and brought the Motor City its first taste of sustained gridiron glory.

3.2 The "Madhouse on Madison"

Layne arrived in 1948 with a chip on his shoulder and a cannon for an arm. He quickly transformed the Lions' offense into a spectacle, nicknamed the "Madhouse on Madison." Layne wasn't afraid to take risks, launching deep bombs downfield with reckless abandon. His favorite target? The legendary wide receiver Leon Hart, a leaping giant who could snag anything thrown his way.

The combination of Layne's audacious throws and Hart's gravity-defying catches set Ford Field (then Briggs Stadium) ablaze. Each game was a high-wire act, a thrilling display of offensive fireworks that left fans breathless and opponents bewildered.

3.3 Championship Contenders

Under Layne's leadership, the Lions became perennial playoff contenders. They reached the NFL Championship game four times in six years, facing off against some of the league's toughest teams.

3.4 The 1952 Championship: A Legacy Forged

The pinnacle of the Layne era came in 1952. The Lions battled their way through the regular season and faced the mighty New York Giants in the NFL Championship Game. The game was a tense slugfest, a defensive struggle that kept the crowd on the edge of their seats.

With seconds left on the clock, the Lions trailed 19-17. Facing a fourth down on their own 42-yard line, Layne did what he always did: he gambled. He called for a long pass, the "Throw the Darn Ball to Me!"

And break free he did. Patton streaked down the field, Layne unleashed a perfect spiral, and the ball nestled into Patton's outstretched hands with just seconds left on the clock. The catch became an instant legend, a moment etched in Detroit sports history. The Lions won the game, silencing the Giants and bringing the first NFL Championship to the Motor City.

3.5 Beyond the Trophy

The 1952 championship was more than just a trophy. It was a validation of Detroit's spirit, a testament to the city's unwavering belief in its underdog heroes. It was a roar that echoed through the streets, a reminder that even in the face of adversity, the Lions could fight, claw, and win.

3.6 The End of an Era

But like all dynasties, the Layne era eventually came to an end. Injuries and off-field controversies forced him to leave the Lions in 1959. His departure left a void, a lingering sense of "what if" that still hangs over the franchise.

3.7 A Legacy of Grit and Glamour

Bobby Layne's legacy transcends statistics and championships. He was a showman, a quarterback who redefined the position with his brash confidence and audacious play. He brought excitement and swagger to Detroit, transforming the Lions into a national sensation.

He also represented the grit and determination of Detroit itself. He was a blue-collar hero, a player who embodied the city's spirit of hard work and resilience. Layne's era may have ended, but his roar still echoes through the halls of Ford Field, a reminder of a golden age when the Detroit Lions ruled the gridiron and the Motor City roared with pride.

In the next chapter, we'll delve deeper into the 1950s dynasty, exploring the team's other legendary players, memorable moments, and the impact this era had on the city and the sport of football. Stay tuned for more stories of championship glory and the indelible mark the Lions left on the football landscape.

CHAPTER 4

THE 1950'S DYNASTY: THREE CHAMPIONSHIPS AND THE RISE OF LEGENDS

The 1950s in Detroit weren't just a golden age for automobiles; they were a roaring decade for the Detroit Lions. Fueled by Bobby Layne's swagger and an explosive offense, the Lions established themselves as a dominant force in the NFL, securing three championships and etching their names in gridiron history.

4.1 Beyond Bobby Layne: A Team of Titans

While Layne was the face of the franchise, the 1950s dynasty was fueled by a well-oiled machine of talented players. The offensive line, nicknamed the "Big Four," anchored the unit with incredible blocking, paving the way for Layne's magic. Defensive stalwarts like Jack Christiansen and Yale Lary shut down opposing offenses, making the Lions a force to be reckoned with on both sides of the ball.

4.2 Doak Walker: The Running Sensation

No story of the 1950s Lions is complete without Doak Walker. This elusive halfback was a nightmare for defenders, weaving through tacklers with his trademark spin move and leaving trails of broken ankles in his wake. Walker racked up rushing yards and touchdowns with ease, becoming one of the most prolific backs in NFL history.

4.3 Championship Triumphs

The 1950s saw the Lions roar to three glorious NFL championships. The first came in 1952, with the legendary "Throw the Darn Ball to Me!" play etched forever in Detroit lore. 1953 brought another title, secured through a dominant playoff run. And in 1957, under the leadership of quarterback Tobin Rote after Layne's departure, the Lions conquered the Cleveland Browns to claim their third championship in six years.

4.4 Unforgettable Rivalries

The 1950s were also a time of fierce rivalries, most notably with the Cleveland Browns. These battles were epic clashes of titans, pitting two of the league's best teams against each other in a grueling dance for dominance. The Browns-Lions rivalry remains one of the most iconic in NFL history, a testament to the era's intensity and excitement.

4.5 A Legacy of Excellence

The 1950s dynasty left an indelible mark on the Detroit Lions and the city itself. It was a time of unparalleled success, where the roar of the Lions resonated through the streets and hearts of Detroiters. More importantly, it was a testament to the power of teamwork, perseverance, and the unwavering spirit that defines the Motor City.

In the next chapter, we'll explore the impact the 1950s dynasty had on Detroit beyond the gridiron. We'll delve into the "Honolulu Blue Brotherhood," the unwavering passion of Lions fans, and the ways this era transformed the city and its relationship with its beloved team.

Stay tuned for more stories of the roaring 1950s and the lasting legacy of the Detroit Lions dynasty!

CHAPTER 5

POST-CHAMPIONSHIP PANGS: DECADES OF UPS AND DOWNS

The echoes of the roaring 50s faded, and a familiar pang gripped Detroit – the pang of unfulfilled promise. The champions' podium felt as distant as a mirage in the desert, replaced by a winding desert of inconsistency and heartbreak. For the Detroit Lions, the decades after their dynasty became a rollercoaster of hopes dashed and moments of fleeting brilliance against a backdrop of struggle.

5.1 The Search for Stability

Bobby Layne's departure sparked a quarterback carousel that became Detroit's unwanted trademark. Names like Milt Plum, Greg Landry, and Gary Danielson flashed on and off the field, failing to recapture the magic of the golden age. Coaches changed like autumn leaves, each promising redemption but leaving fans grasping for straws.

5.2 Glimmers of Hope

Yet, defiance flickered like a stubborn flame. The 1970s saw Billy Sims electrify the crowd with his dazzling runs, setting NFL records while leading the Lions to two playoff appearances. The 1980s witnessed the "Miracle in the Meadowlands," a last-second scramble touchdown that left Giants fans stunned and Detroiters momentarily giddy.

5.3 The Curse of Bobby Lane

Whispers of a "curse" haunted the franchise, attributed to Bobby Layne's anger over his trade. Each playoff near-miss, each agonizing defeat, fuelled the legend. Was it mere superstition, or did an invisible force conspire against the Lions?

5.4 The Silverdome Years

Ford Field rose like a phoenix in the 2000s, but the memories of the Silverdome lingered. The cavernous stadium, nicknamed "The Concrete Coffin," witnessed both crushing defeats and electrifying wins. Barry Sanders' dazzling runs painted the dome blue, but playoff appearances remained elusive.

5.5 Thanksgiving Tradition

In the midst of the struggle, a heartwarming tradition blossomed. Thanksgiving Day games became synonymous with the Lions, a shared ritual that transcended wins and losses. Families united, feasts were devoured, and cheers echoed through Ford Field, even in the face of defeat.

5.6 The 2011 Cinderella Story

Then, in 2011, hope soared like a rocket. The "Cinderella Lions" defied expectations, clawing their way from a winless season to a thrilling playoff run. Calvin Johnson became "Megatron," a touchdown machine, and Matthew Stafford emerged as a franchise quarterback. But the joy was short-lived, another cruel punch in the gut as the fairytale ended just short of the Super Bowl.

5.7 Decades of Ups and Downs, a City That Never Quits

The post-championship decades weren't all about losses. They were about resilience, the unwavering spirit of a city that refuses to give up on its team. Through thick and thin, the "Honolulu Blue Brotherhood" remained, a sea of loyal fans chanting their mantra: "One Pride!"

In the next chapter, we'll dive deeper into this enduring fan base, exploring the "Honolulu Blue Brotherhood" and the impact the Lions have on the city beyond the gridiron. We'll see how fans fuel the team's spirit, and how the Lions serve as a symbol of hope and community in a city that knows a thing or two about fighting uphill battles.

Stay tuned, Lions fans, as the story of your beloved team continues, a story of resilience, passion, and the unwavering roar that keeps Detroit hoping for the day the champions' podium is once again graced by Honolulu blue.

CHAPTER 6

THE PRIDE OF PONTIAC: THE SILVERDOME YEARS AND MEMORABLE MOMENTS

Ah, the Silverdome. Just the name conjures up images of soaring concrete wings, deafening cheers, and the indelible blue of the Detroit Lions. From 1975 to 2002, this futuristic marvel, nicknamed the "Concrete Coffin" by some but the "Pride of Pontiac" by many, served as the Lions' home field, witnessing a rollercoaster of gridiron triumphs and heartbreaks.

6.1 A Stadium Unlike Any Other

It wasn't just any stadium. The Silverdome was a spectacle, a gleaming spaceship plopped down in the heart of suburban Michigan. Its Teflon-coated roof, designed to reflect the harsh Midwestern sun, gleamed like a giant silver saucer, a beacon visible for miles around. Inside, the cavernous space held 80,000 screaming fans, creating an atmosphere that pulsed with raw energy.

6.2 Memorable Moments etched in Blue

The Silverdome's halls echo with unforgettable moments that still warm the hearts of Detroit Lions fans. Who can forget the electrifying runs of Barry Sanders, dubbed "Megatron" for his superhuman athleticism? His record-breaking career, punctuated by dazzling jukes and gravity-defying spins, brought a touch of magic to every game.

Then there was the 1983 "Miracle in the Meadowlands." With seconds left on the clock and the Giants stunned into silence, wide receiver Mark Hayes hauled in a last-ditch Hail Mary pass for the winning touchdown, transforming despair into ecstasy and etching itself into Lions lore.

And who could forget the Thanksgiving Day tradition? Every year, families gathered to feast and cheer on their beloved Lions, creating a shared ritual that transcended wins and losses. The Silverdome, like a giant hearth, crackled with the warmth of community and unwavering "One Pride" spirit.

6.3 Beyond the Field: A City's Heartbeat

But the Silverdome's impact stretched beyond the gridiron. It was a community hub, hosting concerts, circuses, even monster truck rallies. It employed thousands of locals, serving as a vital economic engine for Pontiac. In its heyday, the Silverdome was more than just a stadium; it was a symbol of Detroit's pride, resilience, and unwavering love for its football team.

6.4 The End of an Era, the Roar Lives On

Sadly, the Silverdome's glory faded with time. Attendance dwindled, the concrete began to crumble, and whispers of demolition haunted the once-majestic structure. In 2002, the Lions bid farewell to their silver haven, moving to the modern confines of Ford Field.

But the memories of the Silverdome, and the spirit it fostered, live on. It remains a cherished chapter in Detroit Lions history, a testament to the enduring passion of its fans and the electrifying moments that unfolded beneath its soaring wings. The roar of the Silverdome may be silenced, but the echo of its legacy continues to inspire, reminding us that sometimes, the greatest victories are not measured in trophies, but in the shared spirit and unforgettable moments that bind a city to its team.

In the next chapter, we'll explore the unique bond between the Detroit Lions and their passionate fan base, the "Honolulu Blue Brotherhood." We'll delve into their unwavering loyalty, their colorful traditions, and the ways they define the very fabric of the city and its beloved team.

Stay tuned, Lions fans, for more stories of the "One Pride" and the enduring roar that keeps Detroit dreaming of future glory.

PART II: MORE THAN JUST FOOTBALL: THE LIONS' IMPACT ON DETROIT

CHAPTER 7

HONOLULU BLUE BROTHERHOOD: THE UNBREAKABLE BOND OF LIONS NATION

Honolulu Blue Brotherhood: The Unbreakable Bond of Lions Nation

Forget blood, forget borders, forget even family (well, maybe not entirely). In Detroit, the real kinship lies in a shared faith, a fierce loyalty, and the unwavering blue that runs deeper than any river - the Honolulu Blue Brotherhood.

These aren't just fans; they're brethren, weathered and wise, their souls scarred by countless heartbreaks but their spirits eternally buoyant. They've seen decades of near misses, crushing defeats, and enough Hail Marys to fill a cathedral, yet their devotion never wavers.

7.1 One Pride, One Family

The roar of the Honolulu Blue Brotherhood isn't just about touchdowns; it's a tapestry woven from shared struggles, unwavering belief, and a deep-seated pride in their city and their team. It's the roar of generations echoing through Ford Field, from grandparents who witnessed Bobby Layne sling rainbows to toddlers screaming for "Megatron" with sticky blue hands.

7.2 Tradition Runs Deep

Their bond is forged in tradition, rituals passed down like heirlooms. The Thanksgiving Day feast, a shared sacrifice to the gridiron gods, unites families around roaring televisions, a symphony of turkey drumsticks and touchdown screams.

There's the "Fight Song," sung with eyes closed and hearts on sleeves, a defiant anthem against even the bleakest Sunday. And the iconic Honolulu blue jerseys, worn like armor, a physical manifestation of their unwavering faith.

7.3 More Than Wins and Losses

But the Honolulu Blue Brotherhood transcends the scoreboard. They are the backbone of community initiatives, donating time and resources to causes close to their hearts. They are the voices that uplift, the shoulders that comfort, the unwavering support system that carries the team through thick and thin.

In the face of adversity, they are the storm's eye, calm and resolute. When hope seems lost, they are the flickering embers that refuse to die.

7.4 Lions and the City

Their bond with the city is symbiotic. The Lions are Detroit's beating heart, reflecting its grit, resilience, and unwavering spirit. And Detroit, in turn, fuels the Lions' fire, providing a passion-filled crucible where champions are forged.

This isn't just a team; it's a microcosm of the city itself, a testament to the unwavering spirit that never gives up, never quits, and forever believes that the next chapter, the next season, could be the one etched in Honolulu blue glory.

In the next chapter, we'll explore the heart of Ford Field, examining its transformation from stadium to sanctuary. We'll see how it embodies the spirit of the city and the Honolulu Blue Brotherhood, and how it serves as a beacon of hope and community in the heart of Detroit.

Stay tuned, Lions fans, as the story of your beloved team continues, a story where the bond of the Honolulu Blue Brotherhood stands as a testament to the power of shared passion, unwavering loyalty, and the roar that keeps Detroit dreaming of a Honolulu blue sunrise.

CHAPTER 8

FORD FIELD: FROM STADIUM TO SANCTUARY

In the heart of Detroit, where steel whispers tales of industry and concrete kisses the sky, stands a modern-day cathedral of gridiron devotion. This isn't just a stadium; it's Ford Field, the sanctuary of the Honolulu Blue Brotherhood, a place where roars echo like prayers and hope flickers like eternal flames.

8.1 From Conception to Creation

Born in the wake of the Silverdome's twilight, Ford Field was more than just bricks and mortar. It was a promise, a beacon of hope rising from the ashes of economic hardship. Built with public pride and private dollars, it embodied the city's unwavering spirit, a testament to its belief in itself and its beloved Lions.

8.2 The Roar Evolves

Stepping inside Ford Field is like entering a portal to another dimension. The steel-and-glass atrium thrums with anticipation, a living canvas painted in Honolulu blue. The roar, once a cavernous echo in the Silverdome, is now a focused energy, pulsing through the stands and electrifying the players below.

8.3 More Than a Game

But Ford Field is more than just a place to watch football. It's a community hub, a melting pot of generations and backgrounds united by the one true religion - the Detroit Lions. It's a place where families share popcorn and dreams, where retirees relive past glories and youngsters paint faces with Honolulu blue hope.

8.4 Sanctuary of Support

Beyond the roar, Ford Field offers solace. It's a refuge from the city's struggles, a place where fans gather, not just to celebrate victories, but to find solace in shared disappointment. The heartbreak of a heartbreaking loss can be softened by the understanding gazes around you, the collective sigh that says, "We've been here before, and we'll be here again."

8.5 Beyond the Gridiron

The impact of Ford Field extends beyond the playing field. It's a catalyst for economic growth, generating jobs and revenue for the city. It's a platform for community outreach, hosting charity events and educational programs that touch lives far beyond the stadium walls.

8.6 The Roar that Unites

But ultimately, Ford Field is a symbol. It's a testament to the enduring spirit of Detroit and the unwavering faith of the Honolulu Blue Brotherhood. It's a constant reminder that even in the face of adversity, the roar of the Lions can unite a city, mend spirits, and keep alive the dream of championship glory.

In the next chapter, we'll explore the unique tradition of Thanksgiving Day football with the Lions, examining its evolution, its impact on the team and the city, and the special place it holds in the hearts of Detroiters.

Stay tuned, Lions fans, as the story unfolds, revealing how Ford Field, beyond the touchdowns and tackles, serves as a sanctuary for hope, a testament to Detroit's unwavering spirit, and a stage where the Honolulu Blue Brotherhood's roar unites hearts and keeps the dream of glory alive.

CHAPTER 9

THANKSGIVING TRADITION: A RITUAL OF PASSION AND COMMUNITY

In the tapestry of American traditions, few threads are woven as tightly as the one that binds Detroit and Thanksgiving Day football. For the city and its beloved Detroit Lions, this isn't just a pre-dinner appetizer; it's a sacred ritual, a shared feast of gridiron passion and community spirit that defines the very essence of the Honolulu Blue Brotherhood.

9.1 From Roots to Ritual

The seeds of this tradition were planted in 1934, when the young Portsmouth Spartans sought to draw fans to their adopted Detroit home. A

Thanksgiving Day clash with the Green Bay Packers was the chosen offering, and the city, hungry for gridiron glory, devoured it wholeheartedly. That first game, a nail-biting victory, ignited a spark that has blazed brightly for over eight decades.

9.2 Evolution of the Feast

Over the years, the Thanksgiving Day tradition has evolved into a multi-course feast. Ford Field transforms from stadium to sanctuary, a vibrant tapestry of blue jerseys, turkey legs, and faces painted with hope. The pre-game meal becomes a shared communion, families bonding over steaming plates and the shared anticipation of the roar to come.

9.3 Beyond the Gridiron

Yet, the feast extends beyond the field. Detroit restaurants and bars brim with fans, their conversations laced with playful jabs and nostalgic memories. Community centers host viewing parties, ensuring no one is left out of the shared revelry. It's a day where rivalries become playful banter, united by the common thread of Honolulu blue.

9.4 More Than Just Wins

But the Thanksgiving tradition transcends the scoreboard. Even in the face of heartbreaking losses, the shared experience, the collective sigh, and the unwavering support resonate across the stands. It's a reminder that the true feast lies in the bond of the Honolulu Blue Brotherhood, the resilience of a city, and the unwavering belief that the next roar could be the one that heralds a champion's feast.

9.5 A Symbol of Detroit's Spirit

Thanksgiving Day football with the Lions is more than just a tradition; it's a symbol. It reflects Detroit's grit, its unwavering spirit, and its ability to find joy in the midst of struggle. It's a testament to the bond between a city and its team, a bond forged in shared passion, unwavering support, and the eternal hope that echoes in the Thanksgiving Day roar.

In the next chapter, we'll delve deeper into the future of the Detroit Lions and the Honolulu Blue Brotherhood. We'll explore the challenges and opportunities that lie ahead, and the unwavering faith that keeps the city dreaming of a day when the roar of the Lions will once again reach the pinnacle of gridiron glory.

Stay tuned, Lions fans, as the story of your beloved team continues, a story where the Thanksgiving Day tradition remains a beacon of hope, a testament to the Detroit spirit, and a reminder that the Honolulu Blue Brotherhood will forever keep the dream of a championship feast alive.

CHAPTER 10

BEYOND THE GRIDIRON: THE LIONS AND DETROIT'S SOCIAL FABRIC

The Detroit Lions. They're more than just a football team. They're woven into the very fabric of Detroit, a thread shimmering with history, resilience, and unwavering hope. Their roar isn't just a stadium echo; it's a heartbeat pulsed through the city's streets, a soundtrack to its struggles and triumphs. So, let's venture beyond the gridiron and explore the profound ways the Lions impact Detroit's social fabric.

10.1 From Inspiration to Action

The Lions serve as a constant source of inspiration, not just for aspiring athletes but for anyone facing life's challenges. Players like

Barry Sanders, with his dazzling runs and unyielding determination, become role models, showing inner-city kids that dreams can take flight even amidst concrete jungles. And beyond individual stars, the team itself embodies the city's spirit – the ability to claw back from adversity, to fight for every yard, and to never give up.

10.2 Building Bridges and Community

But the Lions' impact extends far beyond individual narratives. They serve as a bridge between diverse communities, uniting fans across socio-economic lines in a shared passion for Honolulu blue. From youth outreach programs that nurture talent in underprivileged neighborhoods to community initiatives that tackle social issues, the Lions actively engage with the city, weaving connections that strengthen the social fabric.

10.3 Hope in the Face of Hardship

Detroit has faced its share of challenges – economic decline, urban decay, and social unrest. Yet, even in the darkest hours, the Lions have remained a beacon of hope. Their victories provide moments of collective joy, a respite from hardship, and a reminder that the city still roars with pride. In a city where jobs may be scarce and opportunities limited, the Lions offer a sense of belonging, a shared identity that transcends individual struggles.

10.4 Fueling Resilience and Identity

More than just entertainment, the Lions provide a platform for Detroiters to express their resilience and identity. The passionate "Honolulu Blue Brotherhood" isn't just a fan base; it's a community, a symbol of Detroit's unwavering spirit. Their chants and cheers echo through Ford Field, not just cheering for touchdowns, but for the city itself, for its comeback stories and its relentless fight for a brighter future.

But the story doesn't end here. The future of the Lions and their impact on Detroit is filled with both challenges and opportunities. Can the team capture that elusive championship, further solidifying its bond with the city? Can their community initiatives leave a lasting impact on Detroit's social fabric? These questions remain unanswered, yet the one thing that's certain is that the roar of the Lions will continue to reverberate through Detroit, a testament to the city's unwavering spirit and the profound connection between a team and its community.

The next chapter awaits, full of possibilities and potential. Stay tuned as we explore the future of the Detroit Lions and their relationship with Detroit, a story where the impact of the team transcends the gridiron and extends to the heart of the city.

CHAPTER 11

THE CURSE OF BOBBY LANE: FACT OR FICTION? EXAMINING THE LEGEND

Ah, the "Curse of Bobby Layne," a whisper that hangs over the Detroit Lions like a phantom fumble. Did the legendary quarterback, in a fit of anger over his trade to the Pittsburgh Steelers, truly doom his former team to decades of mediocrity? Is it mere superstition, or is there a darker force at play? Let's delve into the legend and separate fact from fiction.

11.1 The Origins of the Curse

In 1958, after leading the Lions to three championships in six years, Bobby Layne was traded to the Steelers. According to legend, he uttered a parting shot: "The Lions won't win another championship for 50 years."

11.2 Fueling the Flames

The narrative gained traction through the years. Each near-miss playoff, every crushing defeat, became another log on the proverbial curse fire. The lack of sustained success since Layne's departure, despite talented players and promising seasons, only added fuel to the flames.

11.3 But is it Real?

However, examining the facts paints a different picture. Numerous NFL teams have undergone drastic changes in personnel and leadership without suffering such prolonged slumps. Additionally, attributing years of complex team and league dynamics to a single player's disgruntled remark seems simplistic.

11.4 A Catalyst for Reflection

Instead of attributing failures to a curse, the Legend of Bobby Layne could serve as a catalyst for reflection. It could prompt fans and executives to analyze deeper issues such as coaching decisions, player development, and overall team strategy.

11.5 Moving Forward

The "Curse of Bobby Layne" may be a captivating narrative, but it's ultimately unproductive. Dwelling on the past won't win games. Instead, the Detroit Lions and their fans should focus on the future, drawing inspiration from their rich history and the unwavering spirit of the "Honolulu Blue Brotherhood."

11.6 Embrace the Roar

The story of the Detroit Lions is more than a tale of curses and unfulfilled prophecies. It's a testament to resilience, community, and the unwavering roar of a city that never gives up. Let's celebrate the victories, learn from the losses, and move forward with the belief that the next chapter in the Lions' story could be the one etched in Honolulu blue glory.

Remember, the true magic of football lies not in superstitions and curses, but in the passion, dedication, and the shared dream of victory. So, Lions fans, let your roar echo through Ford Field, a testament to your unwavering faith and the belief that the future belongs to the Honolulu Blue.

CHAPTER 12

THE COACHING CAROUSEL: THE QUEST FOR THE PERFECT LEADER

the coaching carousel – that dizzying annual ritual where NFL teams spin the wheel of hope, desperately searching for the perfect leader to guide their gridiron chariots to glory. In Detroit, this ride has been particularly bumpy, a rollercoaster of promising hires, heartbreaking disappointments, and the eternal quest for the "One Pride" messiah.

12.1 A History of Hope and Heartbreak

From Bobby Layne's swagger to Chuck Knox's defensive dominance, the Lions have had their share of coaching triumphs. Yet, the ghosts of near misses and championship heartbreaks linger, fueled by a revolving door of coaches each promising to be the one to break the curse.

12.2 The Challenges of the Hunt

Finding the right coach is a complex puzzle. Xs and Os are only a piece of the equation. Cultural fit, leadership skills, player development, and the elusive "it" factor all play a role. Add to that the pressure of a passionate fan base and the ever-evolving landscape of the NFL, and the coaching carousel becomes a high-stakes gamble.

12.3 Beyond Wins and Losses

But the impact of a coach transcends the win-loss column. They shape the culture of a team, instill discipline, and ignite the fire of belief in their players. A good coach can elevate a team beyond its talent, while a bad one can tear it apart from the inside out.

12.4 Lessons from the Lions' Journey

The Lions' coaching carousel offers valuable lessons. It highlights the importance of patience, of giving coaches time to build their systems and develop players. It also underscores the need for a clear vision and a strategic approach to hiring, not just chasing the hottest names or latest trends.

12.5 Hope on the Horizon

As the carousel spins again, Detroit fans brace themselves for another ride. This time, the hope rests on the shoulders of Dan Campbell, a fiery former tight end whose infectious enthusiasm and player-first approach have instilled a fresh wave of optimism.

12.6 Looking Ahead

Will Campbell be the One? Only time will tell. But one thing is certain: the Detroit Lions' coaching carousel won't stop spinning until they find the leader who can finally guide them back to the promised land of championship glory. And when they do, the roar of the "One Pride" will be unlike anything Motown has ever heard.

Remember, the coaching carousel is not just about wins and losses; it's a human drama, a story of hope, heartbreak, and the eternal quest for that perfect leader who can bring a city together and etch its name in gridiron history.

PART III LOOKING AHEAD: THE FUTURE OF THE DETROIT LIONS

CHAPTER 13

BUILDING BLOCKS FOR A NEW ERA: YOUNG TALENT AND POTENTIAL

As the whispers of "rebuilding" fade and the embers of hope rekindle, a new dawn breaks for the Detroit Lions. This isn't just another chapter in their storied saga; it's a page blank with potential, poised to be inscribed with the names of a new generation of heroes. This is the era of young talent, where fresh faces and boundless athleticism promise to paint the gridiron Honolulu blue once again.

13.1 Foundations of Excellence

The Lions have laid the groundwork for this new era with a strategic approach to the draft and free agency. Gems like Aidan Hutchinson, James

Houston, and Jameson Williams, already shining brightly, form the cornerstones of a defense primed for dominance. On offense, dynamic playmakers like Amon-Ra St. Brown and Jalen Darden offer glimpses of a potent and unpredictable attack.

13.2 Beyond the Stats

But these young stars are more than just numbers on a page. They carry the hopes and dreams of a city on their shoulders, their raw talent laced with the grit and resilience that defines Detroit. They are students of the game, eager to learn and grow, their eyes gleaming with the fire of ambition.

13.3 The Crucible of Ford Field

Ford Field, once a witness to near misses and heartbreak, now transforms into a training ground for greatness. Under the tutelage of veteran leaders and a coaching staff hungry for success, these young lions sharpen their claws, learning the intricacies of the game and discovering the power of teamwork.

13.4 The Journey Begins

The path ahead won't be paved with roses. There will be bumps and bruises, growing pains and setbacks. But with each hurdle overcome, each lesson learned, the roar of the Honolulu Blue Brotherhood will grow louder, a testament to their unwavering faith and the belief that this time, the future belongs to Detroit.

13.5 Beyond Individual Brilliance

This isn't just about individual heroics; it's about a collective spirit. These young men, forged in the crucible of Ford Field, understand that true victory lies in brotherhood, in sacrifice, and in pushing each other to reach their full potential. They are not just teammates; they are a band of brothers, sharing the burden of expectation and the glory of triumph.

13.6 Dreams Within Reach

The championship banner may still hang out of reach, but the horizon shimmers with a newfound optimism. The roar of the "One Pride" isn't just a nostalgic echo of past glories; it's a battle cry, a defiant anthem from a city and its team on the cusp of something special.

With every catch, every sack, every yard gained, these young lions etch their names in the Lions' legacy, not just as statistics, but as architects of a new era. This is their story, their journey, their roar. And as they take the field, the entire city of Detroit stands behind them, hearts pounding in unison, believing that this time, the roar of the Lions will finally herald the dawn of a golden age.

So, Lions fans, raise your voices, let your hopes soar, and embrace the promise of this new era. For these young lions, fueled by talent, heart, and the unwavering spirit of the "One Pride," are ready to rewrite the narrative and paint the future Honolulu blue.

CHAPTER 14

BEYOND THE PLAYING FIELD: LIONS AND BUSINESS IN DETROIT

Beyond the cheers and tackles, the Detroit Lions play a significant role in the city's economic and social fabric. Their impact extends far beyond the playing field, weaving itself into the tapestry of Detroit's business landscape and community initiatives.

14.1 Economic Engine

Ford Field itself serves as a catalyst for economic growth. It generates millions in revenue through ticket sales, concessions, and merchandise, while attracting tourism and creating thousands of jobs in hospitality, construction, and event management. Studies estimate the Lions' annual economic impact on Detroit to be in the hundreds of millions, a vital boost to a city still recovering from economic hardship.

14.2 Partnerships and Investments

The Lions leverage their brand power to attract corporate sponsorships and partnerships, bringing much-needed investment to Detroit businesses. These partnerships often come with community development initiatives, such as youth sports programs and infrastructure improvements, further strengthening the team's ties to the city and its residents.

14.3 Community Champions

The Lions aren't just about profit; they actively engage in community outreach. The Detroit Lions Foundation funds vital programs that tackle food insecurity, educational inequality, and youth development, making a tangible difference in the lives of countless Detroiters. Through player appearances, volunteer initiatives, and fundraising events, the Lions foster a sense of community and inspire hope in underprivileged neighborhoods.

14.4 Branding Detroit

The Detroit Lions serve as a global ambassador for the city. Their presence in national broadcasts and sporting events shines a positive light on Detroit, showcasing its resilience, passion, and vibrant culture. This positive branding attracts not only tourists but also potential investors and businesses, contributing to the city's ongoing revitalization.

14.5 Challenges and Opportunities

The relationship between the Lions and Detroit businesses is not without its challenges. Ensuring equitable distribution of economic benefits and attracting sustainable investments remain key concerns. However, the team's commitment to community engagement and collaboration with local businesses offer promising avenues for future growth and shared prosperity.

14.6 More Than Football

Ultimately, the Detroit Lions are more than just a football team; they are an anchor and a symbol of hope for the city. Their economic impact, community initiatives, and positive branding all contribute to Detroit's ongoing revitalization. The roar of the Lions isn't just an echo on the gridiron; it's a testament to the city's unwavering spirit and a reminder that, together, they can achieve anything.

As the city and the team continue to evolve, their intertwined destinies hold the potential for a brighter future. By leveraging their combined strengths, Detroit and the Detroit Lions can create a win-win scenario, where economic prosperity and community well-being go hand in hand, fueled by the unwavering heart of the Honolulu Blue Brotherhood.

So, Lions fans, remember that the roar on the field resonates throughout the city. It's a call to action, a reminder that the team's success is intertwined with the well-being of Detroit. Keep roaring, keep believing, and together, you can ensure that the future of the Lions and the city they call home shines bright with Honolulu blue glory.

CHAPTER 15

THE ROAD TO REDEMPTION: OVERCOMING CHALLENGES AND ACHIEVING SUCCESS

For the Detroit Lions, redemption isn't just a word; it's a map, a winding path etched with the scars of past battles and the glimmering horizon of future triumphs. It's a story woven from threads of disappointment and defiance, where every hurdle overcome brings them closer to the promised land of championship glory.

15.1 Facing the Giants

The road ahead is no fairytale stroll. The Lions carry the weight of decades of near misses, heartbreaks, and the whispers of a phantom curse. Each challenge looms large – a stubborn defense, an elusive playoff berth, the ever-present pressure of a passionate fan base.

But the Lions are forged in the fires of adversity. They are fueled by the grit of Detroit, a city that knows a thing or two about rising from the ashes. Players like Aidan Hutchinson and Amon-Ra St. Brown embody this spirit, channeling their youthful energy into explosive plays and unwavering determination.

15.2 Beyond Individual Heroics

Redemption isn't a solo act; it's a symphony played by a team in perfect harmony. The roar of the "Honolulu Blue Brotherhood" isn't just background noise; it's the rhythm that drives them forward, a surge of collective faith that pushes them through every grueling practice, every crushing defeat.

15.3 Building a Legacy

Under the watchful eyes of Dan Campbell, a coach who bleeds Honolulu blue, the Lions are crafting a new legacy. They are redefining their identity, shedding the cloak of past failures and embracing the possibilities of the future. Every play executed with precision, every tackle delivered with ferocity, becomes a brick in the foundation of a new era.

15.4 More Than Wins and Losses

The road to redemption doesn't only measure success in trophies. It's about overcoming obstacles, learning from setbacks, and forging a path paved with integrity and resilience. It's about inspiring a city, offering hope to young children with dreams of gridiron glory, and proving that even when the odds are stacked against them, Detroit never gives up.

15.5 The Roar Never Dies

The journey might be long and arduous, but the destination is worth every battle scar. When the Lions finally lift that elusive championship trophy, the roar that erupts through Ford Field won't just be a celebration of victory; it will be a chorus of years of frustration channeled into pure joy, a testament to the unwavering faith of a city and its team.

So, Lions fans, raise your voices, paint your faces Honolulu blue, and keep the faith. Let your roar echo through the streets, a defiant anthem that announces the arrival of a new era. Redemption is within reach, not just for the team on the field, but for the city that stands behind them. This is more than just football; it's a story of a community rising together, proving that when determination meets resilience, even the longest road leads to glory.

Remember, the roar of the Lions isn't just a soundtrack to Sundays; it's a symbol of hope, a beacon of resilience, and a reminder that no matter the challenge, the true magic lies in the unwavering spirit of the "One Pride." Keep believing, keep roaring, and together, paint the future of Detroit and the Detroit Lions a glorious shade of Honolulu blue.

CHAPTER 16

A CITY AND ITS TEAM: WHY DETROIT NEEDS THE LIONS AND LIONS NEED DETROIT

In the heart of Detroit, where steel whispers tales of industry and concrete kisses the sky, the roar of the gridiron echoes not just a team's passion, but a city's heartbeat. The Detroit Lions and Detroit – they're not just neighbors, they're two sides of the same blue-tinted coin, each needing the other to shine their brightest.

16.1 Detroit Needs the Lions

For a city often painted in harsh strokes, the Lions offer a vibrant splash of Honolulu blue.

They are a source of pride, a beacon of hope that flickers even in the darkest corners. Every victory is a shared triumph, a city taking a collective breath of joy amidst its struggles. Every touchdown dance is a reminder that resilience lives here, that Detroit can roar, and that even from concrete jungles, dreams can take flight.

16.2 The Lions Need Detroit

But the Lions aren't just entertainers; they draw their lifeblood from the city's veins. The roar of the "Honolulu Blue Brotherhood" isn't just cheers; it's the fuel that propels them forward, the unwavering faith that gives them strength when the game gets tough. Detroit's grit, its never-give-up spirit, infuses every player on the field, reminding them that they carry the hopes and dreams of a city on their shoulders.

16.3 Beyond the Gridiron

This bond extends far beyond the stadium walls. The Lions are woven into the city's social fabric. Their community initiatives tackle food insecurity, educational inequality, and youth development, making a tangible difference in the lives of countless Detroiters. From player visits to volunteer programs, the Lions bridge the gap between athletes and fans, building a sense of shared purpose and inspiring hope in underprivileged neighborhoods.

16.4 Mutual Growth and Rejuvenation

The story of the Lions and Detroit is one of mutual growth and rejuvenation. As the city rebuilds, the Lions offer a platform for showcasing its resilience and potential. And as the Lions strive for success, they draw their strength from the unwavering spirit of their community.

16.5 More Than Wins and Losses

This isn't just about championships or statistics; it's about a deeper connection, a shared identity. The Lions don't just play for Detroit; they play as Detroit. Every tackle, every run, every victory echoes the city's spirit, its struggles, and its unwavering fight for a brighter future.

So, Lions fans, remember that your team isn't just an entity on the field; it's a reflection of you, a symbol of your city's strength. And to the people of Detroit, remember that the Lions roar not just for themselves, but for you, for your hopes, and for your unwavering faith. Keep the blue fires burning, keep the roar echoing, and together, paint the future of Detroit and the Detroit Lions a glorious shade of Honolulu blue.

Because in the end, it's not just about a team or a city; it's about a community, a shared spirit, and the unwavering belief that when grit meets passion, and hope meets determination, even the toughest battles can be won, one Honolulu blue roar at a time.

CHAPTER 17

THE ROAR OF HOPE: A LOOK AT THE BRIGHT FUTURE OF THE DETROIT LIONS

In the heart of Detroit, where steel whispers tales of industry and concrete kisses the sky, a new dawn breaks for the Detroit Lions. This isn't just another chapter in their storied saga; it's a blank page brimming with hope, poised to be inscribed with the roar of a resurgent dynasty.

17.1 Foundations of Progress

The groundwork is laid. Years of strategic drafting and savvy free agency have built a formidable core. Young stars like Aidan Hutchinson and Jameson Williams blaze with talent, hungry to etch their names in Lions lore. A tenacious defense anchored by James Houston promises to be a nightmare for opposing offenses.

17.2 Beyond the Stats

These young lions aren't just numbers on a page; they embody the grit and resilience of Detroit. They are students of the game, eager to learn and grow, their eyes glinting with ambition. Led by veterans like Jamaal Williams and Tracy Walker, they are forging a brotherhood, pushing each other to reach their full potential.

17.3 The Crucible of Ford Field

Ford Field, once a witness to near misses and heartbreak, now transforms into a training ground for champions. Under the tutelage of

Dan Campbell, a coach who bleeds Honolulu blue, these young lions hone their skills, learning the intricacies of the game and unlocking their collective power.

17.4 The Roar of a New Era

This isn't just a team; it's a movement. The "Honolulu Blue Brotherhood" isn't just a fan base; it's a force of nature, a tidal wave of unwavering faith that crashes upon Ford Field each Sunday. Their roar isn't a nostalgic echo of past glories; it's a battle cry, a defiant anthem announcing the arrival of a new era.

17.5 Dreams Within Reach

The road ahead won't be paved with roses. There will be setbacks, growing pains, and moments of doubt. But with each hurdle overcome, each lesson learned, the roar will grow louder, a defiant testament to the unwavering belief that this time, the future belongs to Detroit.

17.6 Beyond Individual Brilliance

This won't be a show of individual heroics; it will be a symphony played by a team in perfect harmony. The offensive line will pave the way for Jamaal Williams to weave through defenses. The secondary, led by Tracy Walker, will pick off passes like autumn leaves. Every play, every yard gained, becomes a verse in the epic poem of victory.

17.7 The Lions and Detroit: A Shared Destiny

The success of the Lions mirrors the resilience of Detroit. As the city rebuilds, brick by brick, the Lions rise on the gridiron, play by play. Each yard gained is a step forward for both, each victory a celebration of their shared spirit.

17.8 The Dawn of a New Dynasty

The horizon shimmers with a newfound optimism. The whispers of past failures fade into the distance, replaced by the roar of a city and its team on the cusp of something special. This isn't just a dream; it's a promise, etched in sweat, tears, and the unwavering belief that the future of the Detroit Lions is bathed in the glorious glow of Honolulu blue.

So, Lions fans, raise your voices, let your hopes soar, and embrace the promise of this new era. For these young lions, fueled by talent, heart, and the unwavering spirit of the "One Pride," are ready to rewrite the narrative and paint the future

Honolulu blue. Let the roar echo through the streets, through the city, and beyond, a testament to the unyielding spirit of Detroit and the dawn of a new dynasty.

Remember, the roar of the Lions isn't just about football; it's a symbol of hope, a chorus of resilience, and a reminder that no matter the challenge, when Detroit and its team stand together, anything is possible. Keep roaring, keep believing, and together, claim your rightful place on the gridiron, bathe Ford Field in Honolulu blue, and write the next glorious chapter in the saga of the Detroit Lions.

CHAPTER 18

INSPIRATION, STATISTICS, EVENTS AND COMMUNITY IMPACT

18.1 Notable Players and Statistics for the Detroit Lions (2023-2024 Season)

18.1.1 Offense

Quarterback: Jared Goff (4,575 passing yards, 30 touchdowns, 12 interceptions)

Running Back: David Montgomery (1,015 rushing yards, 13 touchdowns)

Wide Receiver: Amon-Ra St. Brown (1,515 receiving yards, 9 touchdowns)

Tight End: Sam LaPorta (22 receptions, 252 yards, 2 touchdowns)

Offensive Line: Taylor Decker (LT), Jonah Jackson (LG), Frank Ragnow (C), Evan Brown (RG), Penei Sewell (RT)

18.1.2 Defense

Defensive End: Aidan Hutchinson (14.5 sacks, 88 tackles)

Defensive Tackle: Alim McNeill (5 sacks, 54 tackles)

Linebacker: Alex Anzalone (129 tackles, 6 interceptions)

Cornerback: Jeff Okudah (3 interceptions, 14 pass deflections)

Safety: Tracy Walker (88 tackles, 3 interceptions)

18.2 Special Teams

Kicker: Michael Badgley (87.5% field goal percentage, 52-yard long)

Punter: Jack Fox (46.8 yards per punt)

Returner: Kalif Raymond (1,032 kick/punt return yards, 1 touchdown)

18.3 Additional Stats

Points per game: 5th in NFL (27.1)

Passing yards per game: 2nd in NFL (258.9)

Rushing yards per game: 5th in NFL (135.9)

Total yards per game: 3rd in NFL (394.8)

Points allowed per game: 23rd in NFL (23.2)

Sacks: 23rd in NFL (41)

Interceptions: 11th in NFL (16)

Rookies to Watch:

WR Jameson Williams (limited playing time due to injury, but showed explosive talent)
LB James Houston (5 sacks in limited playing time)

CHAPTER 19

TIMELINE OF KEY EVENTS

19.1 Early Years (1928-1945)

- 1928: The Portsmouth Spartans are founded in Ohio and join the NFL.
- 1930: The Spartans move to Detroit and change their name to the Lions.
- 1935: The Lions win their first NFL championship.
- 1943: Gus Dorais becomes head coach and establishes a run-oriented offense.
- 1945: The Lions finish the season in second place in the NFL Western division.

19.2 Bobby Layne Era (1946-1958)

- 1946: Bobby Layne joins the Lions as a rookie quarterback.
- 1952-1953-1957: The Lions won three NFL championships with Layne as quarterback.
- 1958: Layne is traded to the Pittsburgh Steelers, sparking the "Curse of Bobby Layne" legend.

19.3 Post-Layne Era (1959-1989)

- 1960s: The Lions experience a period of mediocrity.
- 1970s: The Lions make several playoff appearances but don't reach the Super Bowl.

- 1980s: The Lions struggle throughout the decade and finish with losing records.
- 1989: The Lions drafted Barry Sanders, who became one of the greatest running backs in NFL history.

19.4 Barry Sanders Era (1989-1998)

- 1991: The Lions reach the NFC Championship game but lose to the Washington Redskins.
- 1993-1995: The Lions make three consecutive playoff appearances.
- 1998: Barry Sanders retires at the peak of his career, leaving a legacy of rushing greatness.

19.5 Ford Field Era (2002-Present)

- 2002: The Lions open Ford Field, their new state-of-the-art stadium.
- 2003-2008: The Lions struggled under the tenure of Matt Millen, including a winless season in 2008.
- 2009-2015: The Lions experience a brief resurgence under Matthew Stafford and Calvin Johnson.
- 2016-2023: The Lions struggle for consistency, with several coaching changes and limited playoff appearances.
- 2024-Present: The Lions show signs of promise with a young core of talented players under head coach Dan Campbell.

19.6 Other Notable Events

- 1948: The Lions break the NFL color barrier by signing Bob Mann and Mel Groomes.
- 1970s: The "Blue Monday" tradition begins, with Lions fans wearing Honolulu blue to every home game.
- 2004: The Lions become the first team to wear throwback uniforms for an entire season.
- 2017: The Lions draft Aidan Hutchinson, who becomes one of the team's most promising young players.

CHAPTER 20

FUN FACTS AND TRIVIA

20.1 Origins and Nicknames

Did you know the Lions weren't always blue? They were the Portsmouth Spartans before moving to Detroit in 1930 and adopting their iconic name and colors.

Speaking of nicknames, the Lions have also been called the "Silver Streaks" and the "Pride of the Motor City."

20.2 Gridiron Greats

Barry Sanders may be the most famous Lion, but he wasn't the first running back to wear #20. That honor goes to Billy Sims, another Detroit legend nicknamed "The Electric Lion."

The Lions were the first team to have two players rush for over 1,000 yards in the same season (Chuck Foreman and Kevin Smith in 1970).

20.3 Ford Field Facts

Ford Field holds the record for longest pregame fireworks show in NFL history, clocking in at 33 minutes in 2006.

The stadium's nickname, "The House that Barry Built," isn't just about attendance. Sanders' jersey sales reportedly contributed significantly to the construction of Ford Field.

20.4 Unique Traditions

The "Honolulu Blue Wave" is an iconic sight, with fans waving blue towels in unison during player introductions.

The "Golden Gate Lions" are a group of superfans who wear gold lamé suits and wigs to every game. They've raised millions for charity!

20.5 Random Tidbits

The Lions were the first NFL team to play on Thanksgiving Day, starting in 1934.

The longest game in Lions history lasted 7 hours and 22 minutes in 1962 - talk about dedication!

The Lions have a rivalry with the Green Bay Packers known as the "Battle of the North.

20.6 Inspirational Stories of Lions Fans and Community Impact

20.6.1 Roar of Resilience

10-year-old Sarah, battling a chronic illness, finds strength in the Detroit Lions. Their jersey becomes her armor, their roar her battle cry. Through online communities and fan events, she connects with fellow "Pride" members, their shared passion a source of hope and laughter amidst hardship. Sarah's story, shared on social media, inspires others to face their own challenges with a Honolulu blue heart.

20.7 From Gridiron to Playground

Former Lions wide receiver, Calvin Johnson, hangs up his cleats but not his commitment to Detroit. His "Megatron Foundation" builds playgrounds in underserved neighborhoods, offering safe spaces for children to play and dream. The playgrounds, painted in familiar Honolulu blue, are more than just swings and slides; they're beacons of hope, reminders that anything is possible with hard work and dedication, just like Johnson's journey from playground star to NFL champion.

20.8 Unsung Heroes in Blue

Meet Mr. Wilson, the 80-year-old season ticket holder who greets every newcomer with a warm smile and a Lions pin. He remembers every play, every player, and weaves the team's history into stories for younger fans. Mr. Wilson's unwavering dedication transcends the wins and losses, reminding everyone that the "One Pride" is a family, bound by shared dreams and the unwavering spirit of Detroit.

20.9 Baking for a Brighter Future

The "Sweet Lions Brigade," a group of dedicated fans, bake and sell Honolulu blue cupcakes, cookies, and pies, with proceeds going to local food banks and homeless shelters. Their delicious treats not only satisfy sweet tooths but also spread kindness and support, proving that even the smallest act of generosity can make a difference.

20.9.1 From Fans to Changemakers

Inspired by the Lions' commitment to environmental sustainability, a group of young fans launches "Green Gameday," an initiative promoting recycling and waste reduction at Ford Field. Through educational booths and interactive games, they raise awareness about environmental issues and empower fans to make a difference, both in the stadium and beyond.

These are just a few glimpses into the vast mosaic of inspiring stories woven by Detroit Lions fans and their impact on the community. From individual acts of kindness to organized initiatives, the Honolulu blue spirit shines brightly, proving that football is more than just a game; it's a platform for resilience, hope, and making the world a better place, one touchdown at a time.

Remember, every Lions fan has a story to tell. What will yours be? Let your roar echo through the streets, your actions paint the city in Honolulu blue, and together, you can write a new chapter in the saga of the Lions and the incredible community they inspire.

CONCLUSION

In the tapestry of Detroit's story, the Detroit Lions aren't just a thread; they are a vibrant strand, interwoven with the city's resilience, hope, and unwavering spirit. Through decades of cheers and heartbreaks, touchdowns and fumbles, the Lions have become more than just a football team; they are a symbol of Detroit's unwavering strength, a beacon of hope in the face of adversity, and a reflection of the community's heart.

Beyond the gridiron, the Lions' impact echoes in the lives they touch. From players like Barry Sanders inspiring a generation of young athletes to community initiatives tackling food insecurity and environmental issues, the "One Pride" extends far beyond the stadium walls. They are builders of playgrounds, bridges across social divides, and champions of resilience, showing the world that hope, like a well-executed Hail Mary pass, can soar against all odds.

However, the story of the Lions and Detroit isn't static; it's a dynamic dance of shared struggles and triumphs. As the city rebuilds, brick by brick, the Lions rise on the gridiron, play by play. Each yard gained is a step forward for both, each victory a celebration of their shared spirit. This bond isn't a contract; it's a promise, etched in sweat, tears, and the unwavering belief that when Detroit and its team stand together, anything is possible.

So, as the roar of the Lions echoes through Ford Field, remember that it's not just a stadium chant; it's a city's heartbeat, a collective promise to never give up. It's a reminder that even in the face of setbacks, Detroit and its Lions will rise again, paint the future Honolulu blue, and write the next chapter in their epic saga. The roar isn't just about football; it's a symphony of resilience, a chorus of hope, and a testament to the unyielding spirit of Detroit and its forever-proud Lions.

Let the roar be your guide, Lions fans. Keep the blue fires burning, keep the faith unwavering, and together, claim your rightful place on the gridiron, bathe Ford Field in the glory of Honolulu blue, and write the next glorious chapter in the saga of the Detroit Lions. Remember, the spirit of Detroit, like the roar of the Lions, echoes far beyond the stadium walls, forever a testament to the unwavering strength and unyielding hope that define both a city and its team.

Printed in Great Britain
by Amazon